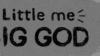

Little me
BIG GOD

Steph Williams

T0034994

STORIES
about
JESUS

Eight True Stories from the Bible

Little Me, Big God: Stories About Jesus
© Stephanie Williams, 2024

Published by:
The Good Book Company

thegoodbook
COMPANY

thegoodbook.com | thegoodbook.co.uk
thegoodbook.com.au | thegoodbook.co.nz | thegoodbook.co.in

ISBN: 9781784989842 | JOB-007564 | Printed in India

Eight True Stories from the Bible

Contents

The house that went SPLAT!

A story Jesus told

Are you good at listening?

LOTS of people listened to Jesus.
He told us about God's love for us
and how to love God and other people.

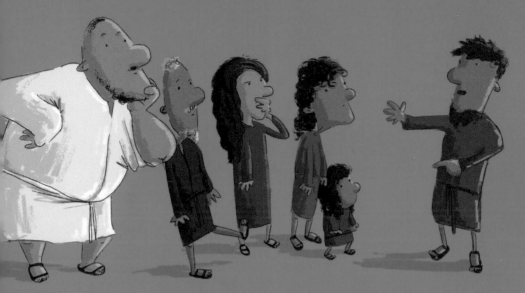

Some people **LISTENED** to what Jesus said,

but they didn't DO it!

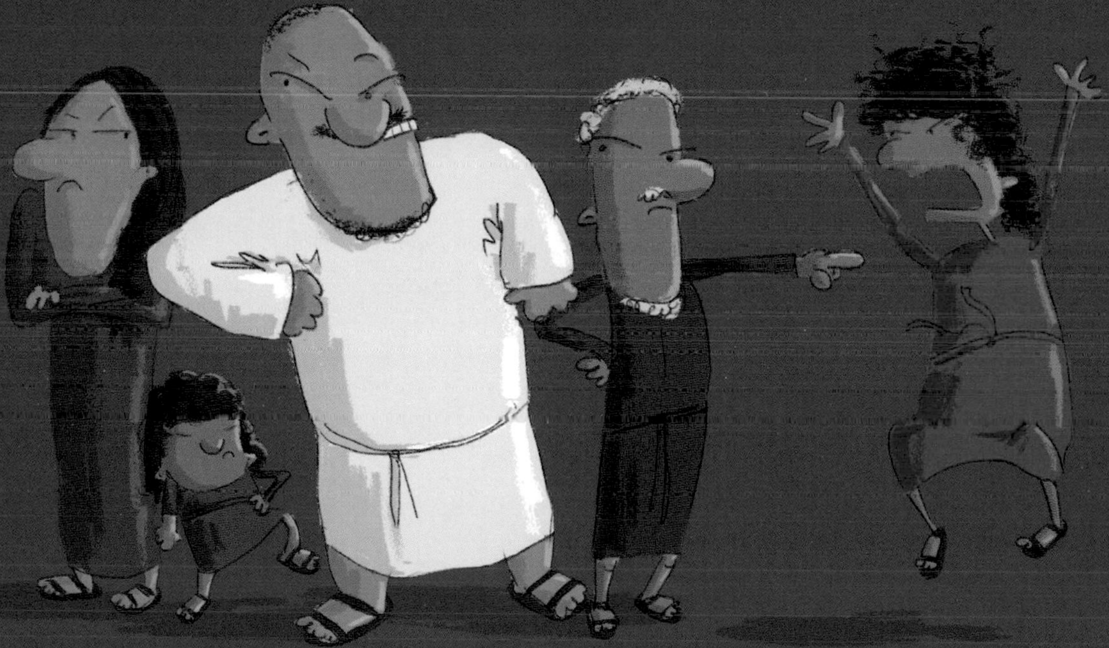

So Jesus told this story ...

Everyone who listens to me,
   AND does what I say, is like a clever man

who built his house on big, **STRONG** rocks.

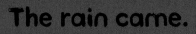

The rain came.

D
r
i
p

splash.

splosh,

POUR!

A flood came. **WHOOOOOSH!**

The wind blew hard.

Wooooooooooooooooooo

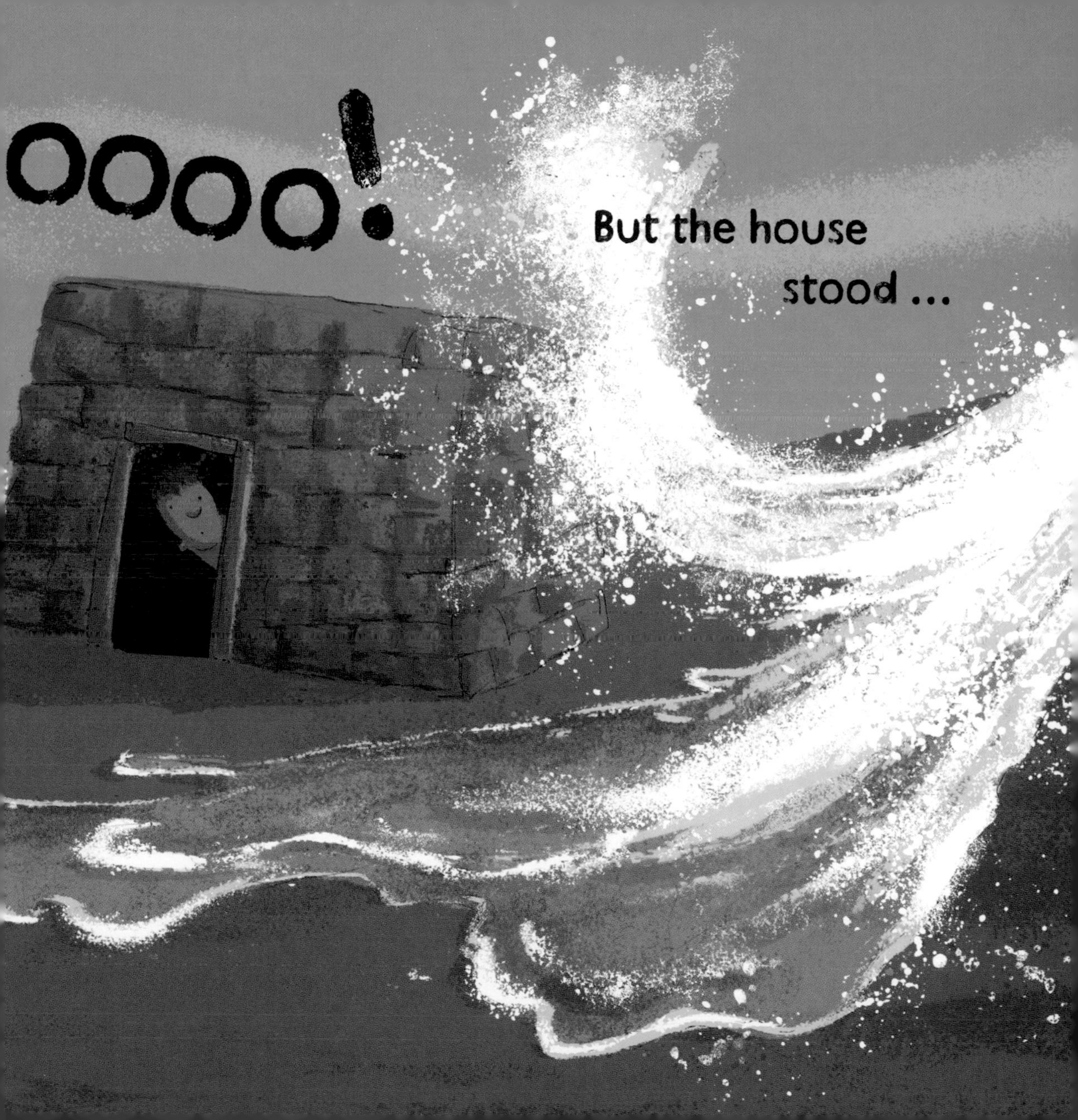

OOOO!

But the house
stood ...

still.

Phew!
Those GREAT **BIG** rocks
made it strong.

But Jesus said, "Anyone who listens to me, but does **NOT** do what I say,

is like a silly man ...

who built his house on soft, loose sand.
Uh oh!

The rain came.

Drip,

splash,

splosh,

POUR!

A flood came. **WHOOOOOSH!**

The wind blew hard.

WOOOOOOOOOOOOOOOOO

OOOOOOO!

And the house
went ...

AT!

And what a big splat that was!

If we don't care about what God says,
we end up in a terrible mess.

But if we listen to Jesus
and do what he said,
we will be safe in God's care
for ever.

Notes for older readers

You'll find this story Jesus told in the Bible in Matthew chapter 7, verses 24 to 27 (or you can read it on the next page). Jesus told the crowds how to follow God and love others. Some people seemed to listen and called him their "Lord", but they did not really care about doing what God wants and did not do what Jesus taught. Jesus warned that when these people expect to be welcomed into God's world in heaven, he will tell them he never knew them. (This is in Matthew 7 v 21-23.) After saying this, Jesus told this story about the two builders—the first builder, he said, is like people who listen and respond to his words, and the second builder is like people who listen but don't do anything in response.

So what does it mean to listen to Jesus and do what he says? We all do things that Jesus says break God's rules—like being selfish or proud or getting angry with people. We don't always do what Jesus says. When we hear Jesus's teaching on what it means to truly love others, the right way to respond is to recognise that in our lives we have not always done this. We need to ask God for forgiveness and we need to ask him to help us live with him as the real King in our lives.

To say that we are fine as we are, or to believe in God without it having an effect on our lives, is like building a house on the sand. If we genuinely want to follow God, we will want to live the way Jesus teaches, trusting in God's help and forgiveness. This will show in our actions, and we will have the rock-solid security of a real friendship with God.

Matthew 7 v 24-27

(Jesus said) [24] "Therefore everyone who hears these words of mine and puts them into practice is like a wise man who built his house on the rock. [25] The rain came down, the streams rose, and the winds blew and beat against that house; yet it did not fall, because it had its foundation on the rock. [26] But everyone who hears these words of mine and does not put them into practice is like a foolish man who built his house on sand. [27] The rain came down, the streams rose, and the winds blew and beat against that house, and it fell with a great crash."

The boy who SHARED his SANDWICH!

Jesus and his friends were
very busy helping everyone,

and they were tired!

They found a quiet place
and sat down. Ahhhhhh ...

But who's that?

People! More and more ...

But Jesus cared about the people.

"Where can we get them some dinner?"
he asked Philip. (Jesus knew really!)

"Dinner? For all these people?" said Philip.

"Loads and loads of money could only buy enough for a teeny, tiny bite each!"

"This boy has a sandwich to share,"
Andrew said,

"but it's only two little fish and five pieces of bread. That's not enough!"

How did Jesus do that
with just one sandwich!?

Everyone was amazed, and they all wanted Jesus to be King!

But Jesus said, "You're just thinking about getting your dinner, which is all finished now."

"I've come to give
you something

that's never
finished and
always enough!"

"Didn't you see the amazing things I've been doing? They show you that God sent me ...

so that if anyone in the world
comes to me for help,
and believes in me ...

they can have life that lasts

for ever,

not just for now!"

Notes for older readers

This story comes from John 6 v 5-15 and 25-35. Jesus and his disciples had found a quiet place to rest. When Mark tells this story in his Gospel, he says that Jesus and his followers were so busy helping people that they did not have time to eat (Mark 6 v 31)! Even though Jesus needed a break, he felt sorry for the people who came looking for him. With one boy's five small loaves of bread and two fish, Jesus fed over 5,000 people.

Jesus' miracles were signs that show us who he is. But the people there that day were not thinking about who could have such power, and they did not see what they needed his help with most. They were just thinking about their food and how Jesus could make their lives better now. So he said, "You are looking for me, not because you saw the signs I performed but because you ate the loaves and had your fill. Do not work for food that spoils, but for food that endures to eternal life" (John 6 v 26-27).

Jesus told the crowd that he had come to give them something much, much better: "Whoever comes to me will never go hungry, and whoever believes in me will never be thirsty" (v 35). He had come to this world so that anyone who believes in him will have life for ever, in heaven with God.

John 6 v 5-35

5 When Jesus looked up and saw a great crowd coming towards him, he said to Philip, "Where shall we buy bread for these people to eat?" 6 He asked this only to test him, for he already had in mind what he was going to do. 7 Philip answered him, "It would take more than half a year's wages to buy enough bread for each one to have a bite!" 8 Another of his disciples, Andrew, Simon Peter's brother, spoke up, 9 "Here is a boy with five small barley loaves and two small fish, but how far will they go among so many?"

10 Jesus said, "Make the people sit down." There was plenty of grass in that place, and they sat down (about five thousand men were there). 11 Jesus then took the loaves, gave thanks, and distributed to those who were seated as much as they wanted. He did the same with the fish. 12 When they had all had enough to eat, he said to his disciples, "Gather the pieces that are left over. Let nothing be wasted." 13 So they gathered them and filled twelve baskets with the pieces of the five barley loaves left over by those who had eaten. 14 After the people saw the sign Jesus performed, they began to say, "Surely this is the Prophet who is to come into the world." 15 Jesus, knowing that they intended to come and make him king by force, withdrew again to a mountain by himself. ...

25 When they found him on the other side of the lake, they asked him, "Rabbi, when did you get here?" 26 Jesus answered, "Very truly I tell you, you are looking for me, not because you saw the signs I performed but because you ate the loaves and had your fill. 27 Do not work for food that spoils, but for food that

endures to eternal life, which the Son of Man will give you. For on him God the Father has placed his seal of approval." ...

[35] Then Jesus declared, "I am the bread of life. Whoever comes to me will never go hungry, and whoever believes in me will never be thirsty."

Jesus was coming to dinner!

And Martha was

busy, busy, busy ...

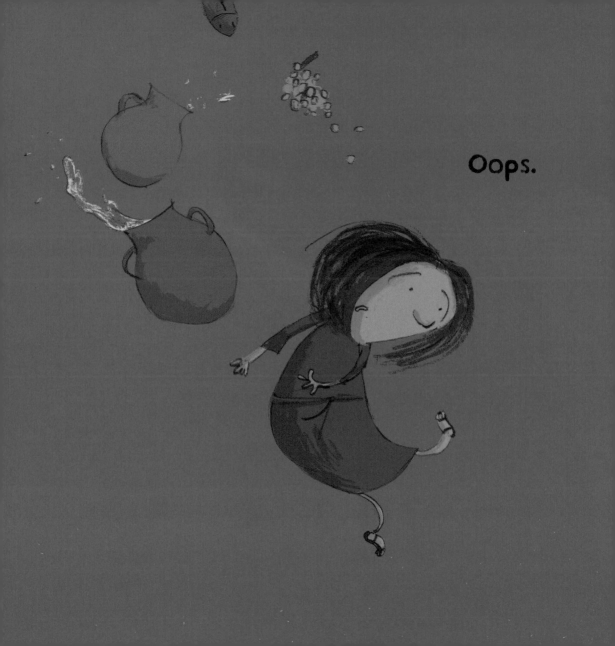

Oops.

But Mary ...
	where was Mary?

Not in the kitchen.

Not in the hall.

Mary was not busy at all!

There she is, just sitting down still -
listening to Jesus!

"Not helping one bit!"

said Martha.
"Hmmmmmphhhh!"

"Tell her to help!"
Martha said.

But Jesus didn't do that.

He said, "Martha, Martha,
you're all in a flap!"

"But there's only one thing
that really matters."

"You just need to listen to me, like Mary."

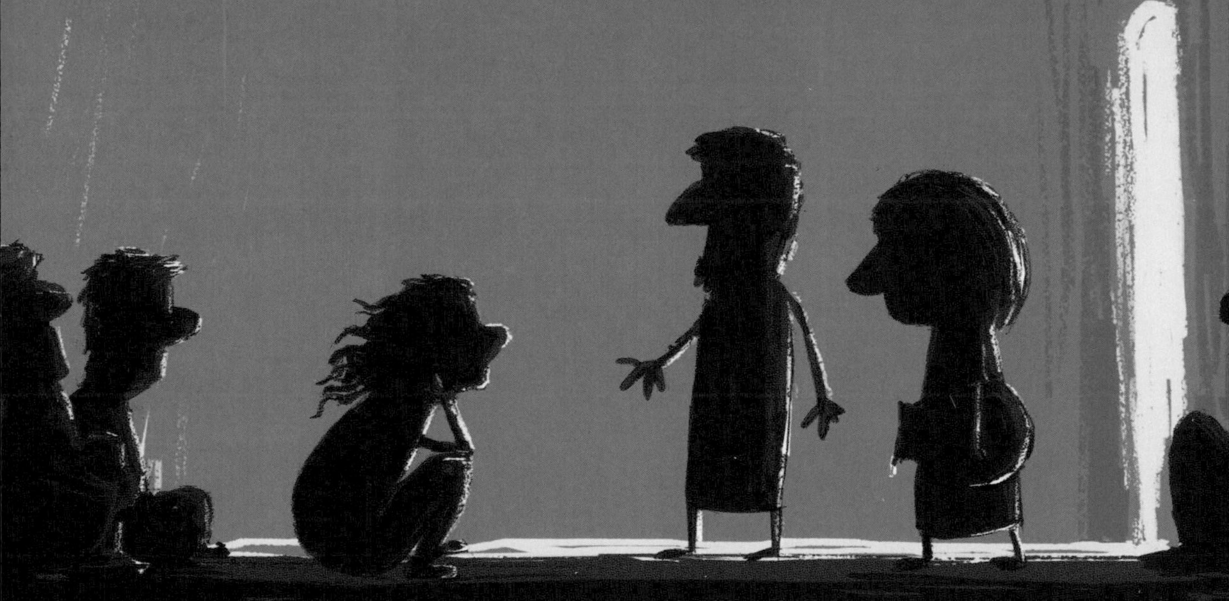

And we can listen to Jesus too.

Because listening to him
is the best thing to do!

Notes for older readers

This story comes from Luke 10 v 38-42. Mary and Martha, and their brother Lazarus, were all friends of Jesus. When Jesus came to visit their home, the two women acted very differently. Mary sat at Jesus's feet listening to him, but Martha was rushing around getting everything ready for their guest.

When Martha saw that Mary wasn't helping, she complained to Jesus, "Lord, don't you care that my sister has left me to do the work by myself? Tell her to help me!" (v 40).

But Jesus told her that Mary had made the best choice: "Martha, Martha," he said, "you are worried and upset about many things, but few things are needed—or indeed only one. Mary has chosen what is better, and it will not be taken away from her" (v 41-42). Mary realised how important Jesus was. She understood that she didn't need to serve and help him as much as she needed to listen to him and receive his help.

Listening to Jesus is always the best thing to do!

Luke 10 v 38-42

[38] As Jesus and his disciples were on their way, he came to a village where a woman named Martha opened her home to him. [39] She had a sister called Mary, who sat at the Lord's feet listening to what he said.

[40] But Martha was distracted by all the preparations that had to be made. She came to him and asked, "Lord, don't you care that my sister has left me to do the work by myself? Tell her to help me!"

[41] "Martha, Martha," the Lord answered, "you are worried and upset about many things, [42] but few things are needed—or indeed only one. Mary has chosen what is better, and it will not be taken away from her."

"Some people say a great BIG,

LOUD prayer,

so **EVERYONE** sees and everyone
thinks they are so good!

"Some people say a really

loooooooooooooooooo

ong prayer, with **LOTS** of fancy words that don't really mean **ANYTHING!** Blah, blah, blah ..."

Don't be like them.
God loves you like the best Dad ever.

He knows what you need
- with NO words!

So when you pray, do it like this ..."

First, Jesus said we
should start with God:

"God, our SUPP

R-Dad

in heaven,

may EVERYONE see how good and kind and right you are!"

And then we can talk
about other people:

"Please can **YOU**
be King in our world?

Help people to do the things you want,
                        like in heaven!"

And then we can
talk about us!

"Please give us the things we need today.

We're sorry we've done things that are not good or right.

Please forgive us.

We forgive everyone who has
done something wrong to us.

Please help us be good.
Please keep us safe.

Amen."

How come we can talk to GOD
like he's our Dad!?

Because Jesus made it so
we can be in God's family.

Why don't you talk to him today?

Notes for older readers

This story contains a well-known prayer that Jesus taught his followers, called "The Lord's Prayer". It is found in Matthew 6 v 5-13. Today, people often pray the exact words of this prayer, and that's great! But we know from what Jesus said just beforehand that it is the meaning of the words that is important, not the exact words we use.

Jesus used two examples of people praying to explain that we cannot earn God's help by using special words or saying long prayers. And prayer is not something we should do to look good to God or to other people. No, if we are followers of Jesus we really can just talk to God as our loving Father in heaven when we pray!

How could Jesus say that we can talk to God like this? Because he had come to fix things between us and God, so that we can be God's greatly-loved children. Because of Jesus, we can know the perfectly good, almighty God, enjoy his love and blessings for ever, and speak to him now in the way that Jesus taught.

Matthew 6 v 5, 7-13

[Jesus said,] [5] "And when you pray, do not be like the hypocrites, for they love to pray standing in the synagogues and on the street corners to be seen by others. Truly I tell you, they have received their reward in full ... [7] And when you pray, do not keep on babbling like pagans, for they think they will be heard because of their many words. [8] Do not be like them, for your Father knows what you need before you ask him.

[9] "This, then, is how you should pray:
"Our Father in heaven,
hallowed be your name,
[10] your kingdom come,
your will be done,
on earth as it is in heaven.
[11] Give us today our daily bread.
[12] And forgive us our debts,
as we also have forgiven our debtors.
[13] And lead us not into temptation,
but deliver us from the evil one."

The dad who NEVER gave up

A story Jesus told

Once there were two brothers.

The little brother asked their Dad
to give them **ALL** his money.

He took his half of the money
and went a long, long way away ...

and he used it ALL up
buying nice things,
ALL for himself!

Soon he had no more money
and no more food.

No food for breakfast,
no food for lunch,
no food for dinner.

He was so hungry, he
wanted to eat pigs' food!

Yuck!

Then the little brother
remembered something.

"My Dad has lots of food, but I wasn't nice to him."

"I don't think I can be his boy anymore.

I don't think he will want to be my Dad anymore."

"But maybe, if I'm very sorry, and I work for him, he'll give me some food."

So he went all the way home.

But the little brother was wrong.

As **SOON** as his Dad
saw the little brother ...

... he ran up the road,

and gave him a

great,

BIG ...

... GINORMOUS hug.

The little brother started to say sorry.

He started to say that he was too bad to be part of the family anymore.

But he never finished,
  because his Dad was shouting,

"Everyone! Let's have a party!
I've found my little boy!"

The big brother was grumpy,

"Why are you giving
HIM a party?
HE wasn't nice to you!"

"I was good.
I worked hard.
You didn't give
ME a party."

"You can always have my things,"
said the Dad, "and you always have **ME.**"

"But your little brother was
lost and we've found him,
so we had to have a party!"

Did you know that you and me are like the little brother? We've gone away from God and not listened to him.

Sometimes we're not kind and don't share.

But God loves us like the Dad who never gave up loving his little boy!

God forgives and helps anyone who trusts in him.

It's not because
we're so good ...

It's because
it's because God's
love is so **BIG**!

Notes for older readers

This story that Jesus told comes from Luke 15 v 11-32. He told it to some religious leaders who were cross because he was making friends with people who were not very good (Luke 15 v 1-2).

These religious leaders thought that, by obeying lots of religious laws, they could please God. The people they called "sinners" had broken these laws in a way that everyone could see. But inside, the religious leaders' hearts were also far from God. They did not love others, which is the very thing that Jesus says all of God's laws are based on (Matthew 22 v 36-40).

Like the older brother in the story, the religious leaders proudly thought they could earn God's reward. But they didn't see that God's love is free and undeserved—the kind of love that forgives the lost younger brother. They didn't see that God was offering to be their heavenly Father. Jesus came to welcome us back into friendship with God. He came to find us and show us that we have walked away from God in the way we have lived, and that we need to come back to him. We can do this by simply asking God for help and forgiveness, like the little brother asked his dad. Then we can know God as our loving Father and look forward to spending for ever in his heavenly home.

Luke 15 v 11-32

[11] [Jesus said] There was a man who had two sons. [12] The younger one said to his father, "Father, give me my share of the estate." So he divided his property between them.

[13] Not long after that, the younger son got together all he had, set off for a distant country and there squandered his wealth in wild living. [14] After he had spent everything, there was a severe famine in that whole country, and he began to be in need. [15] So he went and hired himself out to a citizen of that country, who sent him to his fields to feed pigs. [16] He longed to fill his stomach with the pods that the pigs were eating, but no one gave him anything.

[17] When he came to his senses, he said, "How many of my father's hired servants have food to spare, and here I am starving to death! [18] I will set out and go back to my father and say to him: Father, I have sinned against heaven and against you. [19] I am no longer worthy to be called your son; make me like one of your hired servants." [20] So he got up and went to his father.

But while he was still a long way off, his father saw him and was filled with compassion for him; he ran to his son, threw his arms round him and kissed him.

21 The son said to him, "Father, I have sinned against heaven and against you. I am no longer worthy to be called your son."

22 But the father said to his servants, 'Quick! Bring the best robe and put it on him. Put a ring on his finger and sandals on his feet. 23 Bring the fattened calf and kill it. Let's have a feast and celebrate. 24 For this son of mine was dead and is alive again; he was lost and is found." So they began to celebrate.

25 Meanwhile, the elder son was in the field. When he came near the house, he heard music and dancing. 26 So he called one of the servants and asked him what was going on. 27 "Your brother has come," he replied, "and your father has killed the fattened calf because he has him back safe and sound."

28 "The elder brother became angry and refused to go in. So his father went out and pleaded with him. 29 But he answered his father, "Look! All these years I've been slaving for you and never disobeyed your orders. Yet you never gave me even a young goat so I could celebrate with my friends. 30 But when this son of yours who has squandered your property with prostitutes comes home, you kill the fattened calf for him!"

31 "My son," the father said, "you are always with me, and everything I have is yours. 32 But we had to celebrate and be glad, because this brother of yours was dead and is alive again; he was lost and is found."

Everybody wanted to see Jesus

so he could help them
and pray for them.

Some boys and girls
just like you came to see Jesus.

But Jesus's friends said,
"You're too little."

"Jesus can't talk to you."

And someone said, "Jesus is TOO busy!"

And someone else said,

"Jesus is TOO important!"

And someone else said ...

"STOP!"

"Wait a minute."

"Haaaaaang on ..."

"Let those little ones come here.
STOP getting in their way!"

Who was it?

It was Jesus!

Jesus said,
"You don't have to be a great, big,

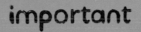

super-good,

important

person

to be God's friend."

"No, no, no!"

"God is friends with you

if you know you are
     just little and need his help."

... is that you?

Notes for older readers

This story comes from Mark 10 v 13-16. The disciples wanted to stop people bringing their children to Jesus, but this is what he said: "Let the little children come to me, and do not hinder them, for the kingdom of God belongs to such as these. Truly I tell you, anyone who will not receive the kingdom of God like a little child will never enter it" (v 14-15).

Jesus wants us to be his friends, and to follow him as King of our lives (that's what "receiving the kingdom of God" means). But you don't have to pay to enter God's kingdom, and you can't earn it by being good. Instead it's like a little child getting a present. It's a free gift.

Jesus welcomes everyone who comes to him like a child and puts their trust in him. Anyone can do that—including little children!

Mark 10 v 13-16

[13] People were bringing little children to Jesus for him to place his hands on them, but the disciples rebuked them. [14] When Jesus saw this, he was indignant. He said to them, "Let the little children come to me, and do not hinder them, for the kingdom of God belongs to such as these. [15] Truly I tell you, anyone who will not receive the kingdom of God like a little child will never enter it." [16] And he took the children in his arms, placed his hands on them and blessed them.

Bartimaeus was sad.

He could not see. His eyes did not work.

But he could hear.

Stomp, stamp, clomp, tramp!

Lots of feet.

And lots of voices.

Jesus was coming!

Bartimaeus opened his mouth
as big and wide as he could and shouted,

VERY

LOUDLY

Jesus!

The best

"Shhhhhh"

"Be quiet!"

"Too loud!"

"Not you!"

everyone said.

But Bartimaeus
was not quiet!

He opened his mouth
even wider

and shouted

EVEN

LOUDER.

And – stomp, stamp, clomp ... stop!

Jesus stopped ...

and called Bartimaeus!

"What do you want me to do?" he said.

"I want to see!" said Bartimaeus.

"You're all better!" Jesus said,
   "You believed in me, so now you can see."

And suddenly Bartimaeus **could** see!

Bartimaeus saw something
no one else could see ...

The King GOD said was coming

... had come!

The King God sent to make things better
... and not just eyes.

And that was someone
worth shouting about!

Notes for older readers

This story comes from Mark 10 v 46-52. Bartimaeus was a blind beggar, but he could see who Jesus really was. He called Jesus the "Son of David", another name for the Christ, the perfect King who God had promised to send, who would be from the family of King David.

So when he called out "Son of David", what Bartimaeus was really saying was "Here is the best King ever, the one who God said was coming!" Bartimaeus believed that Jesus was the promised King and that Jesus could heal him.

"I want to see," he told Jesus. "Go," said Jesus, "your faith has healed you" (v 51-52). Straight away, he could see, and he used his sight to walk along the road with Jesus. Bartimaeus believed in Jesus and followed him. Jesus welcomes everyone who believes in him and wants to follow him.

The story also calls Jesus "the King God sent to make things better… and not just eyes". The Bible tells us that we are separated from God by our sin—the wrong things we do, say and think. Jesus came to make this better. If we trust in Jesus, we can have our sin forgiven and be friends with God for ever.

Mark 10 v 46-52

46 Then they came to Jericho. As Jesus and his disciples, together with a large crowd, were leaving the city, a blind man, Bartimaeus (which means "son of Timaeus"), was sitting by the roadside begging. 47 When he heard that it was Jesus of Nazareth, he began to shout, "Jesus, Son of David, have mercy on me!"

48 Many rebuked him and told him to be quiet, but he shouted all the more, "Son of David, have mercy on me!"

49 Jesus stopped and said, "Call him."

So they called to the blind man, "Cheer up! On your feet! He's calling you." 50 Throwing his cloak aside, he jumped to his feet and came to Jesus.

51 "What do you want me to do for you?" Jesus asked him.

The blind man said, "Rabbi, I want to see."

52 "Go," said Jesus, "your faith has healed you." Immediately he received his sight and followed Jesus along the road.

This is the story of how
God sent someone

to fix everything.

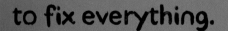

That someone
        was called Jesus.

But some people didn't like
how Jesus fixed things.

They closed their eyes.
They closed their hearts.
They said no to God.

They put Jesus on a cross to die ...

a cross for bad people.

They put his body in a grave
and shut the door tight.
Was it "The End"?

1, 2, 3
days later ...

When Jesus' friends came back,
the big stone door was open!

"Jesus is ...

not here!"

"He's alive! He's all better!"
blinding-bright angels told them.

"Don't you remember? Jesus told you he had to die and come back alive again!"

It wasn't Jesus who said no to God.
It wasn't Jesus who wasn't kind.
It wasn't Jesus who should be
put on a cross.

But

Jesus died

for

us.

Jesus didn't come just to fix a few things.

He gave his life to fix the thing
that makes everything broken ...

our broken friendship with God.

Now anyone
who believes in Jesus

is friends with God.

He came alive again,
to show us how one day, in heaven,
EVERYTHING will be fixed
for God's friends,
for ever.

Notes for older readers

This story comes from Luke 24 v 1-8, but it starts right back at the beginning of the Bible. The book of Genesis (the first book in the Bible) tells us that God made a perfect world but that people disobeyed his rules—they said no to God. They were not friends with God anymore, and because of this, the whole world became broken. Sadness, hatred, illness and death came into our lives; we cannot live for ever anymore. Our broken friendship with God is "the thing that makes everything broken". But someone was coming to fix it!

The Bible tells us that God came into the world as a person, Jesus Christ, with no guilt of his own to pay for. Jesus paid the punishment for when we have said no to God and his rules—the punishment of death, the most broken of brokenness. Now, if we believe in Jesus, we can be friends with God. But Jesus did not stay dead: "He is not here," said the angels by his empty grave (v 6). Jesus came alive again to live for ever and never die, the first person ever to do so. He is like the first fruits on a tree, that shows that a lot of other fruit is about to appear. Jesus coming back to life shows us that the punishment of death was paid, and that God will bring his friends back to life for ever too, in a world that is all fixed.

Some people did not love God, and still said no, closing their hearts to the one God sent. But Jesus welcomes everyone who comes to him and says yes to God. Because of Jesus, we can be friends with God for ever.

Luke 24 v 1-8

[1] On the first day of the week, very early in the morning, the women took the spices they had prepared and went to the tomb. [2] They found the stone rolled away from the tomb, [3] but when they entered, they did not find the body of the Lord Jesus.

[4] While they were wondering about this, suddenly two men in clothes that gleamed like lightning stood beside them. [5] In their fright the women bowed down with their faces to the ground, but the men said to them, "Why do you look for the living among the dead? [6] He is not here; he has risen! Remember how he told you, while he was still with you in Galilee: [7] 'The Son of Man must be delivered over to the hands of sinners, be crucified and on the third day be raised again.'" [8] Then they remembered his words.

Little me
BIG GOD

The whole 10-book series, available individually:

The Little Man Whose Heart Grew Big

The Christmas Surprise

The Dad Who Never Gave Up

The Boy Who Shared His Sandwich

The Easter Fix

The Man Who Would Not Be Quiet

Never Too Little

How Can I Pray?

The House That Went Splat

The Best Thing to Do

thegoodbook.com/lmbg

Bible Storybook for 2-6s

Contains 92 foundational Bible stories, faithfully told and vibrantly illustrated, showing young children how the Bible is one big story from start to finish – the story of God making and keeping his promises. Includes "Promise Icons" to spot, and "Promise Paths" that trace five different promises of God through the narrative of Scripture.

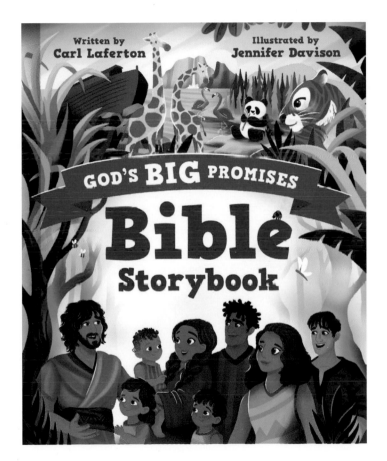

The Very Best Bible Stories Series

Toddlers and preschoolers will have great fun, laugh a lot, and learn more of God's greatness and goodness as you share these engaging and faithful retellings of Old Testament stories with them.

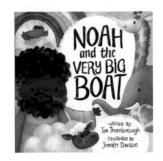

thegoodbook
COMPANY

Little me
BIG GOD